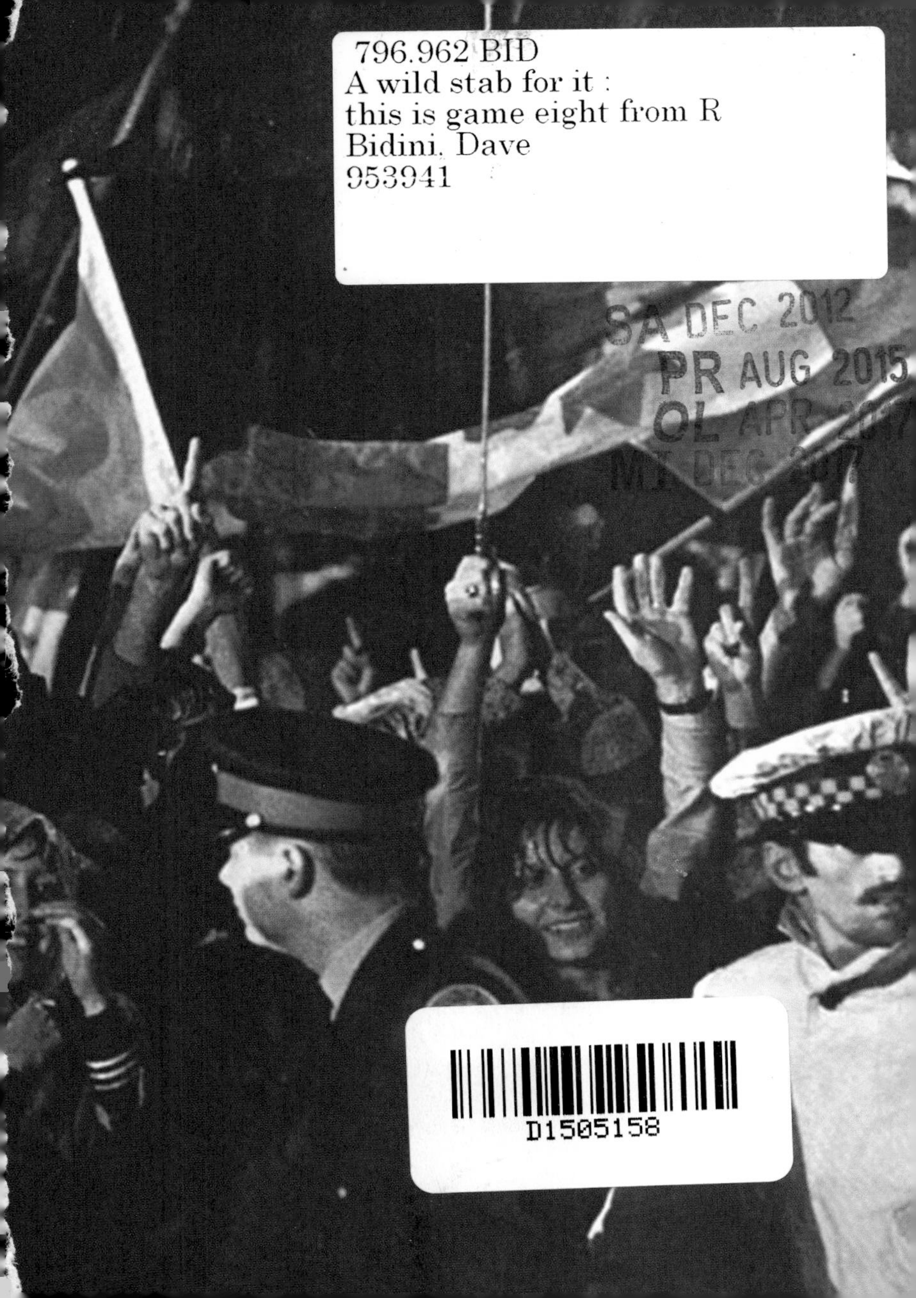

A Wild Stab For It

This is Game Eight from Russia

Dave Bidini

with photos by Brian Pickell

ecw

Published by ECW Press
2120 Queen Street East, Suite 200, Toronto, Ontario, Canada M4E 1E2
416-694-3348 / info@ecwpress.com

Library and Archives Canada Cataloguing in Publication

Bidini, Dave
A wild stab for it : this is game eight from Russia / Dave
Bidini ; photographs by Brian Pickell.

ISBN 978-1-77041-118-0
also issued as: 978-1-77090-319-7 (PDF); 978-1-77090-320-3 (ePUB)

1. Canada-U.S.S.R. Hockey Series, 1972. I. Pickell, Brian II. Title.

GV847.7.B53 2012   796.962'66   C2012-902753-7

Editor for the Press: Michael Holmes
Cover and type: David Gee
Production: Troy Cunningham
Printing: Friesens   5   4   3   2   1

The publication of *A Wild Stab For It* has been generously supported by the Canada Council
for the Arts which last year invested $20.1 million in writing and publishing throughout
Canada, and by the Ontario Arts Council, an agency of the Government of Ontario. We
also acknowledge the financial support of the Government of Canada through the Canada
Book Fund for our publishing activities, and the contribution of the Government of Ontario
through the Ontario Book Publishing Tax Credit. The marketing of this book was made
possible with the support of the Ontario Media Development Corporation.

Canada Council   Conseil des Arts
for the Arts   du Canada

ONTARIO ARTS COUNCIL
CONSEIL DES ARTS DE L'ONTARIO

Printed and bound in Canada

For my teammates, here and there.

**A horse has four legs,
but still, it will stumble.**

— Russian proverb

The lone figure leans in the snow
A rifle is stuck beside him: one hand is on it.

— John Newlove, "Dream"

Sleep

This much we know: the night before Game Eight, Dryden went to bed early. I imagine him fast asleep in his pyjamas, laid flat against a hard, unforgiving Soviet pillow and paper napkin sheets too small for the tall goalie, but his rest was probably more fitful than that: glove hand thrashing and legs kicking at phantom pucks shot into the darkness of his dream. Dryden was down but the rest of the team wasn't, because how could you sleep knowing that when you woke up it would be to face the terrible cackling skeleton of sporting fate staring back at you in a cold mirror of a white hotel room in a strange city on the other side of the world? That's why, when Ted Blackman, the Montreal sports broadcaster, returned to the Hotel Intourist around 11 p.m. after walking the streets of Moscow in the soft late autumn of September 27, he found Team Canada coach Harry Sinden moving through the lobby, his mind soaked in fear and uncertainty, swinging from hope to hopelessness, winning to losing, hero to goat, and back again. Harry unstuffed his hands from his dark blue Team Canada blazer, rubbed his forehead, and appealed to Blackman, "Do me a favour, Ted. Go into the bar and see if any of the players are there. It's past curfew and I don't want to be the bad guy tonight, telling them to go to bed." Blackman said sure, turning towards the tall padded doors of the hotel's lounge. Moments later, he came out. "What's the report?" asked Harry. "Anyone in there?"

"Harry," said Ted, trying not to laugh. "If you could get Dryden out of bed, you could have a team meeting."

War

In the afternoon, they brought us into the gym:
hundreds of children, terrified and hopeful in the
stale air. I was eight years old in 1972. Canada playing
Russia in hockey was unusual in itself, but watching
Canada play Russia in hockey on TV in the afternoon
was stranger still. A friend, Mark Mattson, said, "Back
in those days, the only things you watched on TV in
class were sex education films or religious movies.
So watching hockey, this was really weird."

Before the start of the game, my phys ed teacher —
track-panted in an age when only athletic instructors
wore that sort of thing — barked for us to "Sit Down!"
and "Keep Quiet!" when all we wanted to do was run
around and play tag or war as a way of easing the
thick unbearable tension. We played war because the

'72 series *was* war, or at least that's what Espo said.
We were told that the Russian players — the Soviets
— were trained as soldiers, too, and studied closely,
you could see this in the way their play seemed born
from a strategic operative — zone to zone to zone, a
chalkboard diagram come alive. We were also told that
the players lived on a military camp — a *basa* — where
their athletic corporals allegedly warned them that if
they missed a break-out pass or gave away the puck,
they would be sent to Siberia, which is where I found
myself forty years later, sitting in a kitchen drinking
tea and eating dark chocolate with women who lived
through such times. "It was hard, yes," said one of
them, reapplying her lipstick every few minutes, "but
we were happy, too, in a way. There was fear of what
might happen, but there was also a great feeling of
togetherness." I asked her, "But with the gulags right
here . . . didn't that make it hard for you to believe in
the hope of the future?" Overhearing my question,
one of the women's husbands took me into the living
room, where he pulled out an old map and went region
by region, showing me how strong and mighty the
Soviet Union used to be. "Yes. We were in awe of you;
afraid, too," I told him. Then the man's son showed

up. "But Dad," he said, "back then if your boss treated you badly, there was nothing you could do. If you spoke out, you would be fired, and sometimes, worse." The father rolled his eyes and looked at me. They fought for awhile as I sat on the sofa thinking about a question Espo had once asked, then answered, himself, "Would I have killed to win the series? Yes, I believe I would have." In September 1972, we ignored the gym teacher's cries and kept playing war. Then Mr. Dawson screamed one final time. "Children, THE GAME! It's starting!" We looked up.

Gretzky

In 2004, I was travelling through Tatarstan with a fiftysomething Soviet broadcast employee: a cameraman and sound engineer named Sergei. Whenever an unmarked car would come up behind us, he'd stroke his Van Dyke beard and tell us, "Look: KGB." Once, after we were stopped by police on our way back to Kazan, he added, "This is how they take you. Quietly, out of nowhere." It wasn't until I'd suffered three days of this that I realized he was joking. I played along for his amusement until, one time, our driver noticed a different set of lights in the rearview mirror. He shouted at us to stay quiet. The car pulled up beside ours, and two men spoke to the driver. After discovering that we were from Canada, they asked if any of us were Wayne Gretzky. It was Sergei's turn to laugh. We drove on.

Head Cold

First, there was a shot of an empty ice surface. The transmission came and went, suggesting a fat, jumpsuited technician hitting an enormous metal box with a stick in some studio in Agincourt, trying to bring the pictures back. The shot held for a moment, as if stillness might have somehow calmed the trembling, anxious viewer. Then, there was a voice — part cartoon frog, part leprechaun, part Popeye and part head cold — wobbling like old tape. It was Foster Hewitt, "Tonight we are making hockey history. I wouldn't miss this one for all the tea in China." Then the camera moved slowly, showing the great players marching head down and in two single files along the carpet to the rink. Generally, the Canadians seemed hairier and rounder, and, generally, the Russians were

smaller and blonder, although both teams wore red
and white — or white and red — and had, generally, a
look of duty about them as they stepped onto the soft
ice. There was no pumped-up glove-slapping go-get-
'em histrionics while skating out of a flaming logo;
no small children holding team flags with a song by
U2 filling the arena from speakers dangling around
the circumference of the rink; no grrrrring announcer
rolling his r's as he introduced the teams (home team
loudest; visitors, less so). Instead, the scene was darkly
meditative: a quiet (for now) building and two dozen
players whose look suggested one more long walk
down the weird carpet to the too-warm ice surface,
and one more speech from the coach before one more
long, draining game in this long, draining series. If the
event had forced players on both teams closer to the
hot sight at the centre of their nation's gaze — weaving
them into the fabric of cultural and political history
on the barbed needle of sport — it also made them
question, near the end of the series, who they were
skating for and why. Revisionist poetics tell us that
Team Canada wanted to win for Johnny Frozen Pond
and Uncle Albert back in Adenoid and the writers of
the thousands of letters sent to Russia by Canada Post

— which team assistants used to wallpaper the corridors outside the dressing room — but, more than that, the players wanted to win the series for themselves. Ken Dryden told me, "I knew about Ralph Branca and Bobby Thompson and what had happened to the Brooklyn Dodgers. I knew there would be a goat, and I didn't want to be him." Only a few players could sense the weight of what might happen to their reputations if Canada lost to Russia, but everyone knew that it would be bad. As for the Soviets, they'd been to Montreal; they'd been to Toronto; they'd been to British Columbia. No man could stay the same after doing what millions of their countrymen had only dreamed.

Petals for the Kremlin

After skating a few laps around the rink, the players lined up along their respective blue lines: Canada to the left, Russia to the right. Anthems crackled over the PA — during the music, a slow, ominous shot panned across the thick netting behind the goal, which looked like chain mail or the bars of a cage — before the players were introduced by an announcer whose voice was as soothing as a raccoon squealing down a chimney ("The International Hockey Match between Team Canada and the Soviet Union is declared open!"). Here, the crowd finally announced its presence: 3,000 Canadians — the largest airlift of bodies into Europe since World War II — trying to drown out the Soviet fans' whistling: moose versus bees, hounds versus wasps, walrus versus mosquitos.

When Gary Bergman, the bald, angry uncle of Team Canada's defence, was called, he twirled to the rink's four corners, smirking as he waved V for peace, although the V could have stood for other things, too.

After the introductions, the teams broke. Every Canadian except for the starting six took their place on the bench beside injured defenceman Rod Seiling, who sat at the end wearing a London Fog trench coat. Beside him, Wayne Cashman, Bill Goldsworthy and Dale Tallon paced in their navy team jackets, chewing Trident or Chiclets or Juicy Fruit or Freedent, and, beside them, assistant coach John Ferguson glowered at the ice, his sharp, angry nose pointing like a fuck-you finger at the Russian team. Tretiak, the young Russian goalie, skated to the bench from his crease, where, a few feet to Ferguson's right, the players huddled closely together. From a camera high in the stands, it looked like the closing of damp flower petals. Someone spoke — maybe Yakushev, maybe Lutchenko. They huddled for five seconds, ten. Then the petals opened. Tretiak, all of twenty years old, skated into the loneliness of his crease, where he tapped his pads twice before blinklessly staring forward.

Guitar

Superstar forward Valeri Kharlamov was a deep and soulful man. That's what his teammates said. His mother was half-Spanish, which accounted for his dark features and the way he played the nylon-stringed guitar and sang: beautiful, rich-voiced, emotional. These features might have had him beaten or work-farmed or cast out had he been anything other than an elite, soft-handed and quick-ankled hockey star in the distrustful, racist and xenophobic Soviet Union, but the point was moot because that's what he was. Before he was replaced as coach, Anatoli Tarasov used Valeri as a lynchpin by which he moved the team's triangles of attack, exploiting his killing speed and his ability to improvise, one of the few players afforded such a luxury. While Tretiak and Yakushev would endure to become the lasting hood ornaments of Russian hockey, Kharlamov was something else: a smooth, baby-faced assassin of all that Canadian hockey thought it knew. His emergence was even more startling set against the Western propagandist's view of Russian men: grunting, drunk and piggish, with big fur hats and long rifles hanging from their hips. Instead, Valeri had a Mediterranean nose and dark hair swept across his brow. While visiting Alexander Gusev's apartment in 2005, I noticed a photo of the two men sitting on a hill in the summertime, smiling. Standing alongside his wife, the tall, blond defenceman — then in his fifties — touched the frame and talked about how much he missed his friend, who had died in a highway car crash with his wife in 1981. "That was many years ago, but it seems like yesterday," he said, his voice tightening. His wife added, "A fortune teller foretold this accident to his wife. But no one thought it would happen."

In Game One in Montreal — 7–3 Russia — Kharlamov scored twice. For his first goal, he swept around Don Awrey like a backyard child beyond the reach of a staggering uncle, taking two strides before flicking the puck past Dryden, who stood there as helpless as a scarecrow. Calling the goal, Foster Hewitt

landed hard on the K: "Quite the goal by Kar-la-moff."
By the end of the series, he and the rest of Canada
would get his name right, although there wasn't
much use for it once the series shifted to Moscow.
By Game Six, Team Canada knew that the Russian
forward was favouring his ankle, and so Bobby Clarke
was famously ordered by John Ferguson to tap the
player with vigour, telling him, "That guy is killing
us out there." With a behind-the-ears wind-up, Clarke
shattered Kharlamov's ankle with a single devastating
slash, forcing him to sit out Game Seven. Tarasov's
replacement, Vsevolod Bobrov — who coached while
sitting on a chair at the end of the bench — had no
quick answer for the scoring and speed vacuum
created by Kharlamov's absence. The team was
unprepared for such an important loss, although
it's hard to know how the great Tarasov would have
responded. After all, he believed that violence
degraded hockey, and that, when played finely by the
sport's best skaters, there would be little temptation to
drag the game into a tar pit of cruelty. In Game Six, he
would be surprised how much his theory was tested. In
Game Eight, he would be astonished.

Bandages

Arthur Chidlovski, who lives in Boston and administers the main Summit Series website, was a child growing up in Moscow when the Canadians arrived to play the second half of the series. He said, "At first, the Russian fans thought it would be a series of mutual interest, almost like an exhibition. As a result, it was shocking to see the way Team Canada behaved — running around and arguing like they were part of a comedy routine. I mean, in Russia, we'd never seen a player argue with a referee before. It wasn't done. If you were stopped by a policeman in your car, you wouldn't argue, and we applied this same philosophy to sports." Arthur, who'd been in love with hockey since childhood, wasn't as surprised as others when the series started to become very real and competitive. "The first photo I'd ever seen of a Canadian player was Carl Brewer, taken during the World Championships," he said. "In the picture, most of his face is covered in bandages. It was very shocking to see, not only because of the damage to his face, but because he was so old. In the Soviet Union, players would retire at thirty. And they never had scars. Not like the Canadians."

Dad

Jim Jones was in grade 3 in 1972. All of the teachers were aware that he'd lost his dad a few years before. They'd both been big Dave Keon fans, and in 1970, they sent in enough Coke bottle caps to get Jim a big poster of the Leafs' number 14 for his room. A lot of the kids teased Jim after his dad died, and it was a time of tough lessons taught with tough love. But Jim's teacher, Mrs. Davies, was kind and supportive. So was the school janitor, Mr. Bailey, who was grey-haired, and, Jim said, "probably a grandfather." Jim remembered asking him to fix the chain on his bike and then thinking, "I can't be much of a man if I can't do it alone." But the janitor didn't see it that way. He taught him how to do it.

On the day of Game Eight, the classroom kids

shot their hands into the air the instant Mrs. Davies asked for a volunteer to go to the assembly room in the basement and check the score. They knew the Russians were ahead by two goals thanks to their principal, John Kormos, who'd been updating them on the PA. Mrs. Davies chose Jim. He ran down the worn marble stairs until he found a big black-and-white TV on a six-foot stand with wheels. The sound was blaring. Jim said, "At that moment, I felt very special. The third period was already underway, and I watched alone until Canada scored. Then Mr. Bailey ran in from the boiler room. He had been listening while he worked, I suppose, and we jumped for joy at the tying goal. I remembered my duty and ran back up the four flights to my classroom. Out of breath with excitement, I blurted out, 'We tied it!' Mrs. Davies was the first to head for the door, and everyone else followed in a kind of scramble. Soon, other classrooms followed us. I led the way and found a seat front and centre on the bench. Next thing we knew, Henderson scored. What I remember most is that we were all part of that moment. It was the first time since my dad died that I felt part of anything. It was a lucky day for me and Paul Henderson."

Suomi

In September 1972, Timo Vourisalmi was with his
grandparents on a farm in Toysa, Finland. At the time,
very few people in the country knew anything about
Canadian hockey. Outside of Russia, NHL hockey
was a rumour, if it was anything at all. In 1971, Timo
came across a set of player cards — the Esposito
brothers and Stan Mikita — but because Canada had
withdrawn its teams from the World Championships
and the Olympics, tournaments routinely dominated
by the Russians, he had no point of reference going
into the Summit Series. Timo said, "It was kind of a
thrill to see that NHL players could play at the same
level as the Soviets. If you were a Finnish hockey fan
back then, you hated the Soviet Union and you hated
Sweden, so, of course, I cheered for Canada. There

wasn't much news about the first four games, but when the series moved to Russia, there was lots of talk about them. The special thing about the broadcasts was that it wasn't the usual time of the year for hockey on TV, being so early in the fall. In the 1970s, you saw hockey broadcast during the World Championships every spring; maybe a few national team games
or something from the Finnish league scattered throughout the winter. The players I remember most from the '72 series were the Esposito brothers, Bobby Clarke and the one with the helmet, Paul Henderson. Afterwards, Canadian hockey opened up to us, more so after the start of the WHA and the first Finnish players on those teams."

Bombast

Moments before the beginning of Game Eight
— series tied at three games each — Phil Esposito
— who, despite sweating buckets, seemed to gain
weight and grow larger as the series went on — stood
in the face-off circle waving and gesturing to no one
and everyone, wearing an expression that was part
exasperation and part wonder. If the Russians had
dominated much of the series with their smooth
skating and heaps of skill, Espo filled what was left
with his personality and will. This didn't count for
nothing. As the tournament wore on, the Soviets were
helpless in tamping the behaviour of the Italian-
Canadian forward, and his bombast and fearless self-
assertion left many of his opponents awestruck. Even
though he was hated across the steppe, he was

admired in some corners, too; a poster boy for the
wild freedoms of the West, and someone upon
whom the politburo could not close their lens. In
one sequence of the 1994 film *Anna: 6 to 18*, director
Nikita Mikhalkov describes how, in order to become a
great nation, Russia needed great enemies, cutting in
footage of Espo performing a menacing pantomime
from the penalty box. In Moscow in 2002, the wife
of Yuri Blinov told me how handsome she thought
the Canadian players were and how, after 1972, her
husband chose to wear his hair long because of Phil.
Arkady Tyurin, the director of Russia's homeless
soccer team, said, "Before the series, the Russians had
many words for 'cock.' But afterwards, they called it
only one thing: Esposito. In 1972, he became part of
our language of the streets."

High Rollers and No Hopers

Writer Dave Bist was in Russia for Games Four to Eight. He remembered sitting in a bar when two men came in and settled beside him. "They pulled out some chewing gum and popped it into their mouths," he said, "but after a moment, it became apparent that no one had taught them how to chew gum. They were working it like chipmunks." Bist didn't offer advice because, back then, the locals didn't speak to the visitors unless they were working in an official capacity. Besides, said Bist, "I had hair down to my waist. I looked like no one else in the streets other than some of the other Canadians." Bist remembered coming across a very large man ("He was the size of a duplex," he said) glowering and standing in a doorway. He stared at the long-haired Canadian before he broke into a huge smile, shouting, "Esposito!" It was the Bruin centreman, said Bist, who made the biggest impression him. "You had to be there to realize how wonderful he was. Back-checking like a demon the entire game and scoring huge goals. I've never seen a person work so hard in my life."

Brian Williams, the iconic broadcaster and witness to nearly every important moment in Canadian sport, travelled to Moscow alongside Ralph Mellanby and Dick Beddoes, with whom he roomed. "I'd been there in 1967," said Williams, "so I knew what I was walking into, which is more than I can say for most of the people who came over. Me and Beddoes, we lived on ice cream and champagne and, in a way, it was perfect. I was prepared for things to be different, but I really liked the Russian people. Once, I came down with a chest cold and the great big Russian woman who was in charge of our floor in the hotel invited herself into my room and she rubbed me down, helping me to recover. The people were gracious and they held Canadian hockey in such high regard. You'd get into these great conversations with folks on the street. They'd say, 'Tretiak,' and I'd say, 'Dryden!' and the game would go on from there. We didn't speak the same language, but we knew what each other was saying. For me, that's what the series was about as much as anything."

"I was twenty-six years old at the time," he remembered, "and I was lucky to be hanging around with Beddoes. Every day, he'd hold these press conferences in the lobby, and people would gather around just to listen to him espouse his thoughts on the series, even though no one knew what he was saying. The Russians had never seen anyone dress the way he did: silk scarf around his neck, huge fedora, checkered jacket, wide trousers. Once, he told me, 'Rooms,' — that was my nickname — 'we're gonna find ourselves a racetrack!' So we got on a bus and headed out of town. There was never any control on us, never any restrictions. You should have seen the reaction of people outside the city core to Dick: they were stunned, amused and astonished. He'd tell people, 'I am Canuski!' and their eyes would light up. Eventually, we got to a racetrack way out of town and, sitting there, Dick turned to me and said, 'There are high rollers and no hopers here, too. It's just like being at home.'"

The Next War Will Be Nuclear

Espo finally put his arms down and the puck was dropped. Canada started with the Parise-Esposito-Cournoyer line while Russia countered with Yakushev, Vladimir Shadrin and Vyacheslav Anisin, who'd been promoted from the third line, a.k.a. "The Line from the Mine," featuring three players from Karelia. The teams exchanged harried rushes up the ice, but it wasn't long before the shit started: questionable penalties to Bill White for tripping and Peter Mahovlich for holding not three minutes into the game. Going into Game Eight, the Canadian team — and really, all of Canada — anticipated that Russia would conspire to win the deciding game at all costs, a paranoia fomented by the climate of the times as well as the reputation of the USSR for its sporting brinkmanship. Broadcaster and TSN play-by-play man Gord Miller was seven years old and living in Edmonton in 1972 during the series. Miller said, "We had a Ukrainian neighbour living down the street who'd escaped from the Soviet Union. They'd survived the famine there and he used to talk all the time about how the Soviet Union had raped and pillaged in the Ukraine, about the abuse of little girls — really horrifying stuff. It was also the time of the Cold War, and we were taught to never trust the Russians. One day, there was a headline in the *Edmonton Journal* that said, 'The Next War Will Be Nuclear,' so you really saw the Russians as coming from a hostile place; a place of enemies. During the Olympics in Munich, they'd dominated most sports, and there was almost an underlying hysteria at the start of the series. Because of terrorism and what had happened with the FLQ, we were already living in a climate of fear. School councillors would talk to us about the threat of nuclear war with Russia, and it was something you thought about: how it was more than just a hockey series. Before the drop of the first puck, it felt like war, and once the series shifted to Russia, we thought the Soviets would rig the games as their basketball team had against the USA in the Olympics.

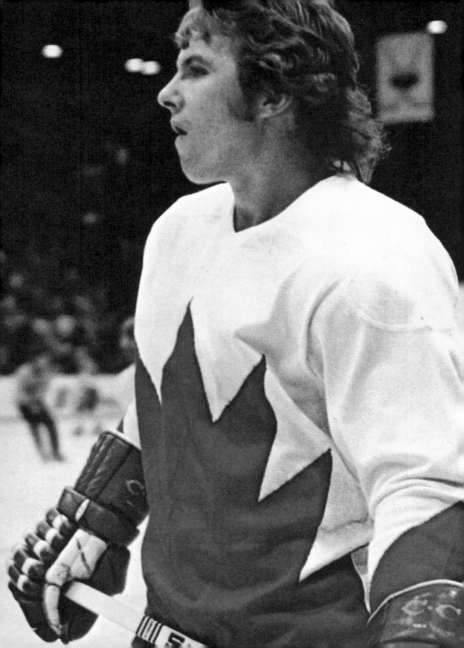

We saw them as deceitful and powerful, and there didn't seem to be any way possible that Canada would come back to win."

As it turned out, these suspicions were confirmed, at least in the early stages of the Russian half of the series. In Moscow, Soviet officials purposefully corrupted Canada's pre-game routine, diet and living conditions. They were denied game-day practice time and access to replacement equipment and skate repair. There were also phone calls to their hotel rooms in the middle of the night and food shipped from home that went missing. Dryden said, "There was a rumour going around that instead of eating chicken, we were eating blackbird." He also talked about being fed small helpings of cheese and sardines for breakfast, and how "you had two dozen or more players who'd done the same game-day routine for countless years, only to have that routine disturbed." Dryden said the team waited the entire series for their shipment of Coca-Cola to arrive, only to find a skid of Jolly Cola from Denmark — brown, weak-bodied, strange-tasting — waiting for them in their dressing room.

It got even worse for Canada when it came to the refereeing. They'd already suffered through Game Six

with Josef Kompalla and Rudolph Batjer ("Bader and
Worse," according to series organizer Alan Eagleson),
who began calling phantom penalties against Clarke,
Henderson and Ellis once it was established that they
were the team's best line. Before Game Eight, Canada
was told by the Russians that the Swedish ref was
sick and the Finn had been called away (or something
like that), leaving them with the controversial pair,
whom Sinden and Ferguson — and really, most of
Canada — saw as untrustworthy and firmly in the
back pocket of Soviet officials. In the beginning of the
final game, quick penalties to White and Mahovlich
immediately raised suspicions, and when Alexander
Yakushev scored on an easy tap-in from the side of
the net — a goal that tied him for the series' scoring
lead with Esposito — Canada's blood seemed set
to boil. After scoring, the Big Yak raised his arms
crooked in the air while Esposito drifted towards the
net, where he leaned on the crossbar and let his head
drop, disgusted at the goal. The Russian fans were
ecstatic, but, in Canada, their cries of joy were only
audible for a moment. After the goal, the televised
image dissolved into a swirl of visual squiggles and
aural burps — the fat, jumpsuited technician hit the

box a little harder — as Foster Hewitt's voice was reduced to a whisper. (Before the series, television consultant Ralph Mellanby advised the production company who broadcast the games to be wary of the audio feed; in his international broadcasting experience, it was always the most precarious aspect to the telecasts.) Soon, a loud hum and bits of static bzzzzzzed like tweezers on an Operation board game, fighting through atmospheric interference not yet scoped for the sort of easy satellite transmission we're used to today. Then came a live announcement from a human voice: "The audio and video trouble we're experiencing is at the Moscow end and it's temporary, so please stand by and do not adjust your set." Something about the way the announcer spoke — calm, quietly authoritative and vaguely patrician — made everyone relax, just so. The trouble in Moscow was only temporary. We were coming back.

Jeeps

When play resumed, there was another penalty, this
time to J.P. Parise. Jean-Paul — a.k.a. "Jeeps" — was
twenty-five when he made the NHL, twenty-eight
before he became a full-timer with the Minnesota
North Stars, playing alongside Jude Drouin and Bill
Goldsworthy. Parise's angular face was like a sharp,
dark arrow, and despite his long, sculpted sideburns
and dashing curl of black hair, there was something
grave about the way he pursued his opponents,
possibly born from the drive and desperation
required to have made the NHL at such an advanced
age. Having survived the intense climate of minor
hockey in the nickel belt of Northern Ontario, and
after kicking around for a half-dozen years in the
backwaters of the AHL, toughness had been drummed

into Parise's play. Along with Wayne Cashman and Dennis Hull, he'd helped get Canada its first series win in Game Two at Maple Leaf Gardens in Toronto. For players like Ken Dryden and Phil Esposito — metropolitans who'd seen their share of scenes and cities and people — skating behind the Iron Curtain would have been stressful enough. But for someone like Jeeps, it would have felt like he'd been shot onto another planet.

Even before the penalty call, Parise seemed angry. In the preceding face-off, he'd circled through the dot like a rabid hound, his menacing stride quickening with each turn. Then, during play, he chopped down a Russian leaving his zone and was called for the infraction. After learning of his fate, he worked himself into an emotional froth. Eventually, he stopped in front of Kompalla and showered him with expletives, barking angrily, his shoulders pinched with rage. Kompalla gave him a misconduct for his language, then Parise skated away, banging his stick on the ice. But Parise turned back. When he did, it was with his Victoriaville raised like a scythe over the referee's head. He brought the stick down and Kompalla crossed his hands in front of his face, bracing himself for impact. Parise stopped the blade less than a foot from the ref's head. The crowd gasped. Serge Savard grabbed J.P. and pointed him to the Team Canada bench, where someone pointed him towards the dressing room. Some have since written how Parise's threat resulted in a capably refereed rest of the game, but as a viewer, and as a kid, to see such

raw and naked emotion played out during the most important game in Canadian hockey history was to be awestruck and unsettled by the adult power of the moment. Some players were affected by this, as well. Frank Mahovlich, the soft-voiced, velvet giant, kicked at the skates of one of the referees, whom he felt was getting too close. Harry Sinden threw a bench onto the ice; John Ferguson whipped a folding chair. At one point, six Canadian players umbrellaed over the referees, shouting at them. Even more remarkably, Parise suddenly reappeared. He skated around the ice, and you could see him contemplating whether or not he should just stay in the game, defying the officials' orders. These strange developments lasted five minutes, ten. Harry threw more stuff and Alan Eagleson came down to talk to the off-ice officials. Colour commentator Brian Conacher told viewers,

"At least a hundred policemen, as well as Red Guards and KGB, have gathered near the bench," and while security is a given in today's arenas, back then any trace of police was unusual and alarming. Eventually, J.P. decided to leave the ice again. He walked past the soldiers, swearing in two languages.

Eventually, the other Canadians moved away from the referees. Across the ice, the blank-faced Bobrov sat looking into the distance like a clerk bored in his chair. The only player who continued to burden the officials was Esposito who, for the next few minutes, stood there talking, talking and talking some more. Genius suggests that he might have been stalling the game so that the Canadians could settle themselves. But the Big Wop probably just never met an argument he didn't like. After play resumed, he lugged the puck into the Russian zone, fought off a handful of players, and immediately tied the game, banking one in off a defenceman. Canada/Russia: 1–1.

Money in the Walls

Gord Miller said, "In 1972, we saw the Russian athletes as genetically engineered supermen, truly bad guys who wanted to take from us that which we adored. After Canada lost 7–3 in Game One, I spent the night in tears. It was very hard to watch. As the rest of the series wore on, my grandfather — with whom I watched the games — was pretty critical of the team. He said the players were playing like dogs, which was the pervasive feeling among adults in Canada. I'm not proud of it, but when Bobby Clarke broke Kharlamov's ankle with the slash, I was happy. I felt that we simply had to beat them, whatever the cost."

"It's all so different now," he said, "but the myth of '72 is still very strong. You notice this during the World Junior tournament, or whenever the two countries meet. This is in spite of the fact that Russian players are everywhere in the West, which is stunning when you think of what it was like after they first arrived to play here. In Montreal, Tretiak remembers the opening reception for the players, and being blown away by how much food there was. It was the same thing for that first wave of players to the NHL; Igor Larionov's wife cried the first time she went into a Safeway in Vancouver. Frank Musil [the defenceman spirited out of Czechoslovakia] couldn't believe it, either. When his agent used a bank machine at the airport, he thought there was money in the walls."

From Baku with Love

In 1972, Dennis Kane watched the series along with
the rest of Canada. He was entranced by the scene
at Luzhniki: anxious soldiers amassed along the
perimeter of the rink, Soviet fans in turtlenecks
studying the action in the dull light, and players in
flowerpot helmets skating beautifully about the ice.

Closer to Moscow, Ludmilla Zorkina watched the
games with her mother — a rifle marksman who also
raced motorcycles — and her grandmother in a small
town near Baku, in Azerbaijan. They found themselves
fascinated by '70s Montreal and the glow of the
beautiful Forum. "We lived in a closed country," she
told me. "We were told that in the USA, nobody could
work and that they were all dying, but we always knew
that Canada was friendly; the people did not create

wars and it was safe there. When we first saw them, we all thought the Canadian players, with their long hair and strong bodies, were very good looking. They were exotic to us, including my grandmother, who loved sports and loved hockey. She used to scream and cheer like crazy at the TV set, and we were all very excited when the series started. During the first game, there was no one in the streets. It was very quiet. Afterwards, we all went wild. It's all anyone talked about the next day at work. After the series, I started to learn English and my dream was to one day go to the Hockey Hall of Fame."

After the series, Dennis moved to Calgary, where he dreamed of visiting the Soviet Union. He read a story by Tim Burke of the *Montreal Gazette* about a member of the Russian chapter of the Montreal Canadiens fan club, so he wrote him, striking up a friendship. After the fall of the Iron Curtain, Dennis and his family went to visit the Russian Habs fan — whose wife was Ludmilla — in St. Petersburg. Over time, he sent Dennis some pins from the Soviet Union — 200 per parcel — and Dennis sold them, eventually raising enough money to bring the couple to Canada for a holiday.

One week before they arrived, Dennis's wife told

him that she wanted to dissolve their marriage. It was a difficult time for both, but they decided to keep up appearances during the Russian couple's visit. When their friends returned to St. Petersburg, Dennis decided to come clean, writing to them and telling them what had happened. He received a letter a few weeks later from Ludmilla, who said that she and her husband had been going through the same thing, but because they wanted so badly to visit Canada, they decided to suspend their breakup. Eventually, Dennis returned to St. Petersburg, where, after a short courtship, he and Ludmilla were married. Today, they live in Powell River, B.C. "It's funny," said Dennis, over the telephone from British Columbia's Sunshine Coast. "The '72 series had such an impact on us that we both wanted to know each other's country. It was our love of hockey — of Canada vs. Russia — that eventually brought us together."

The Impossible Boy

With about ten minutes left to go in the first period,
the puck jumped then fell to rest near centre ice like a
fishing bob hitting the water. Almost immediately, it
was scooped up by the red-helmeted Paul Henderson,
who'd scored Team Canada's two previous game-
winning goals. If a lot of his teammates had seemed
cement-ankled and heavy-hipped next to the skating-
on-air Soviets, Henderson — and perhaps, his Leafs
accomplice, Ron Ellis, as well as Yvan Cournoyer —
played as if he'd stumbled upon a game he'd always
been looking for: one driven by perimeter speed
and puck savvy rather than a shoot-it-in offence
designed to return the puck to the slot. From Game
Five to Game Eight, Henderson moved about the
ice with his tongue wagging and, more than any

other Canadian player, he actually looked like he was enjoying himself, having fun despite the intense pressure and challenging conditions. History tells us that Henderson did what no player in any sport has ever done, at least not at this level of play — score three consecutive game-winning goals in three must-win games — but there was something beyond the benchmarks. He played like a kid on Saturday morning ice, oblivious, it seemed, to the intensity of the circumstances. He also reminded down-at-the-heels Canadians that their game, in the right hands, was about spirit and aplomb and riding the roar of the crowd, too. If the Russians had focused their attention on Espo and Peter Mahovlich and Gilbert and other alien forwards, Henderson's abilities were less threatening because they most resembled theirs. In a way, not only would Team Canada's impossible boy defeat Team Russia almost singlehandedly, he would beat them at their own game, too.

Distant, Fading and Small

Before the end of the first period, Vladimir Lutchenko, who, after glasnost, would end up becoming a longstanding New York Ranger scout, scored on a slapshot during an interference penalty to Yvan Cournoyer, making it 2–1 Russia. The play reflected something Howie Meeker had said: "The Russian defencemen are only defencemen when they haven't got the puck. When they do have it, they're gone." After the Soviets' post-goal celebration — although celebrations were never the '72 Russians' strong suit — the broadcast suddenly froze, only to be replaced by a disembodied Muscovites' hand holding a black card with Lutchenko's name and number on it. (Canadian broadcasting at the time was hardly sophisticated, but Russian State Television made PBS — which showed

the games in the United States — look like Spike TV.)
When the game returned, a crowd of players had
gathered near the boards, where a Russian player lay
prone on the ice beneath Rod Gilbert and Brad Park,
who appeared to have checked him flat. He climbed
to his feet with the help of his teammates, before
hobbling to the bench; even coasting seemed difficult.

It wasn't until we were shown a new camera angle that
we could see who the player was. While he'd missed
the previous game, coaches had put him into the final
on a wing and a prayer, in the process benching the
team's solid, stay-at-home veteran on defence, Rags
Ragulin, who was forced to buy a ticket to watch his
friends play. The fallen player wore number 17. He bent
over at the bench and reached for his ankle, wondering
if it was still there.

Kharlamov.

After the goal, the game opened up. Teams threw
long passes across the ice to players zooming down
the wing and defencemen on both teams carried the
puck more than they had all series, forcing each other
back on their heels. Canada had looked dead-legged
and confused in the first games, but over a half-dozen
games in Europe (including matches in Sweden),

they'd managed to adjust to the Olympic-sized ice. The first time I ever encountered big ice was in Northern China, in Harbin, and, as I've related in *Tropic of Hockey*, looking across to the opposite boards was to see a shoreline thinning on the horizon: distant, fading and small. If it was hard for me — a rec league hacker — to adapt to these dimensions, I can't fathom what it must have been like for players who'd played their entire lives in bandboxes celebrated for their tiny confines: Boston Garden, Memorial Auditorium and Chicago Stadium.

Besides, not only were the Canadian players in poor, summer-cottage shape but, at the beginning of the series, they'd suffered from overconfidence and pro-league Western arrogance. Ralph Mellanby remembered taking Rod Seiling, Bobby Clarke, Paul Henderson, Dale Tallon, Frank Mahovlich, Richard Martin and others to Jamaica that summer on a resort promotion to be shot for the purposes of an intermission segment. He said, "Sitting around the campfire at night, as it were, and after a thousand beers, the guys started talking about how they hoped the series wouldn't be too ugly, how they hoped the scores wouldn't be too lopsided. I tried telling them

that the Soviets could play, but they had no idea
what they were walking into." According to Mellanby,
it wasn't until after Game Five that Harry Sinden
and John Ferguson hatched a plan to exploit the
dimensions of the new rink, a feat for which the two
men have never been recognized enough. "Back then,"
said Mellanby, "there weren't seven assistant coaches
like there are today, so it was really up to those two
guys. I sat with Harry and Fergie after Game Five —
Canada had just played their best hockey of the series,
but still lost — and they broke things down: how the
Russians did what we'd now call 'flooding the zone.' In
the NHL, you picked up your man and that was that,
but the Russians were fast enough and good enough
to send in two forecheckers, and it was killing the
Canadian defence. Back home, players only ever had to
beat one man at a time, and because of the influence
of Bobby Orr, defencemen liked to keep the puck for
a moment before deciding what to do. So what Harry
and Fergie did was to have them ring the puck around
the boards to their wingers as soon as they got it.
When it worked, Canada outnumbered the Russians —
who'd gone too deep — in the neutral zone."

The innovation described by Mellanby didn't

take long to play out, and in Game Eight, it produced
one of the most sublime Canadian goals of the series.
Brad Park ended up finishing the rush, but it was a
four-player effort between Park, Jean Ratelle, Rod
Gilbert and Dennis Hull that resulted in the puck
slipping past Tretiak, who seemed unprepared for
the quickness of the Canadians' play. Racing over the
blue line after a turnover, Park passed to Ratelle who
quickly returned the puck to Park — such deft puck
movement had once been full property of the Russians
— sending the defenceman in on the goaltender,
who shattered Tretiak's five hole. After the goal, the
team swarmed him on the boards, rubbing heads and
locking arms and slapping pants in excitement. It was
the antithesis of how the Russians had celebrated:
congratulating each other in passing before
returning to their stations, heads down. The goal was
a breakthrough for Park, who'd had a rough series
made rougher still considering that he was expected
to fill the shoes of Bobby Orr, who travelled with the
team and practised every day but was too frail to get
into any games. The same was true of Broadway Rod
Gilbert, who Canadian management had hoped would
make up for the goal-scoring absence of Bobby Hull.

Neither player announced themselves until the series moved to Russia, and neither would end up winning a Stanley Cup during their long pro careers. But in Game Eight, Park had already scored a tying goal and Gilbert had taken out Kharlamov. And there was still more to come.

Loves to Pinch

Scotty Bowman first saw the Russians play in the
1950s. In 1966, he was entrusted with having to lead
a Montreal Junior Canadiens team against what
amounted to a version of the Soviet National Team,
men vs. boys, twentysomethings vs. teenagers. "It
wasn't really fair having the two teams play one
another, but before the game, I got a call from Jacques
Plante, who was retired. He told me that he wanted
to play the Russians, so I said, 'Sure.' We were lucky,
because who knows how a young goaltender would
have done against them. Before the game, Jacques told
his defencemen — Serge Savard was on the team, too —
exactly how he wanted them to play and, of course, he
stood on his head. He made something like fifty saves
and we ended up winning the game, 2–1, on a goal with

thirty seconds left by Larry Pleau. Without him, who knows how bad it might have been."

Scotty said, "I knew that the Russians played and trained eleven months of the year. We did the same, but for only for five or six months. Some guys — the Western Canada guys, especially — would go home after the season and work on the farm to stay in shape, and some other guys would work on beer and Coke trucks in the summer, but most players just went up to the cottage. As a result, there was a great physical disparity between countries up until the mid-'80s, so you can imagine what it was like for those guys in '72. I remember when we tested our players on the Canadiens. Guys like Gainey and Lafleur would score in the mid to high sixties on their V/O [lung capacity] tests, but most players were in the fifties; some were even in the low thirties and forties. The Russians were always over seventy. They were machine-like in terms of their fitness. Some of them were quite small, but they had tree-trunk legs and you couldn't knock them off the puck. Back then, they did what we now call 'core training,' so they had a real advantage. The Russians really changed the way we looked at training — at the players' habits and regimen off the ice. I have a grandson who plays hockey in Chicago. He's six years old now and his program is exactly what the Russians were doing from the very beginning: fewer games and more practices, and more focus on the skills so that when kids are ready to play, they're confident and better able to play a team game. In Canada in the summertime, kids played other sports like baseball, but they didn't have that in the Soviet Union. Some burned out before they were thirty, but they were in much better shape to play almost a year's worth of hockey."

Bowman explained that the Russians' strategic genius came in the way they established a puck possession game and the way their ever-moving offence allowed their defence to spread out and cover more ground. "In the early '70s," he said, "NHL defencemen loved to pinch — it was a big part of the team game and it's one of the main reasons why Philadelphia won two Cups — but because the Russians attacked the neutral zone with so much speed, they were caught out of position all the time. When you compare the defencemen's NHL point totals to their point totals in the series, there's absolutely no comparison, and it wasn't until later that

the Canadians were able to adjust and have success
at both ends of the rink. Another difference in the
Russians' play was their wingers, who moved all over
their ice. In the NHL, guys just went up and down the
lane, but the Russian wingers were everywhere. They
were always moving. Always."

Dave Bist remembered, "Before the Russians in
'72, no one had ever seen a player use their skates to
play the puck. It's hard to imagine this not being part
of the game, but it wasn't. The Russians thought of
the game differently. They did things we didn't do,
even though Canada had been playing for twice as
long." Soviet hockey helped develop a myriad of other
innovations: skaters purposefully circling back into
their defensive zone to regroup, something that would
have emasculated goal-hungry Canadian forwards
taught to move simply ahead; wingers and centremen
stopping inside the other team's blue line to set up a
play, a move later mastered by Gretzky, who was ten
years old in 1972; and forwards passing the puck to
where their linemate was skating, as opposed to where
they were. There was also the pre-game huddle, the
humble and workman-like goal celebrations, and the
five-man unit that paired defence combinations with

forwards. Because of the different ways the Soviets moved, it was like forcing the Canadians to read time with the clock hands moving the other way. Before Game Five, Phil Esposito asked broadcaster Ralph Mellanby, "What position does Yakushev play?" Mellanby told him that he played left wing, then asked why Phil wanted to know. Espo said, "I line up against him out there, but I never see him." This mirrored Bowman's words; how it took almost half of the series for Team Canada to notice that Russian forwards played positions other than their own, moving over the ice to meet the demands of whatever play was developing. To say they were disoriented by this is to call a monkey who meets a horse confused.

That said, certain aspects of Canada's game affected the Russians, as well. "The whole mentality of Russian hockey — like Russian life — used to be very methodological," said Arthur Chidlovski. "In Soviet theatre, there was the Stanislavski method — realism above all else — and nothing else. The Soviets liked to stick to one thing, even if that thing could be improved. But after '72, Soviet hockey players realized that you could shoot at the goal more often; you didn't always have to wait for the goalie to be out of position. They also started using the corners more, as opposed to staying away from them at all costs. It was Tsygankov, I think, who asked, 'Must I always pass the puck to someone when coming over the blue line? Why can't I shoot it and go and get it?'" Bowman added, "In 1972, the Russians never took slapshots; they found it to be an ineffective way of shooting the puck. They might have been right, but you look at their players now. You really can't discount any element of the game. In the end, you do whatever you have to do in order to win."

The Faint, Dying Sound

If the Russians of 1972 did help revolutionize a game that, with the exception of Bobby Orr's reimagining of the defence position, had been played the same way for decades, it should be enough to establish them as one of the most influential teams of all time. This pedigree was never more pronounced than in the stirring middle frame of Game Eight in Moscow, one of the strongest and most dynamic overall periods of hockey played by any team.

It started with an early goal in the first minute of play by Vladimir Shadrin (Vlad the Shad) — off a spirited rush by Yakushev — and concluded with Valeri Vasiliev scoring on the power play in the dying minutes. There was another Yakushev goal in the middle — the point pushed him into the series' scoring

lead, one ahead of Esposito — and a mid-period reply
by Canadian defenceman Bill White, with assists from
Ratelle and Gilbert, Canada's best player to that point.
For long stretches, Canada couldn't get near the puck,
even though they were playing their best hockey of the
series. The Russians seemed to toy with them the way
a child teases a cat with a thread of yarn. It was as if
they suddenly remembered what they were doing, why
they were playing, and for whom. After a beautiful rush
by Frank Mahovlich and a subsequent shot from the
high slot by Phil Esposito, Viktor Kuzkin, the veteran
defenceman, recklessly threw himself in front of the
puck, something we hadn't seen before. The Canadians
managed to hold the game at 5–3 for Russia with a
great sequence that produced White's goal, but by the
end of the period, the Big Red machine was playing
as well as it had in all of September. If the whole of
Canada felt sick after the loss in Montreal, fans were
now reaching for their straight razors. At one point,
transmission from Moscow via London broke down
completely and the screen went dark. It was replaced
by a series logo and the faint dying sound of the play-
by-play. Not watching wasn't entirely a bad thing.

The Bleener

Yuri Blinov, who took a regular shift for the Russians
in Game Eight and played wing on the first line
before being replaced by Kharlamov in Montreal,
is a sad, old and beautiful man. On my second trip
to Russia, he was the one legend that I got to know
best, accommodating and gracious to the nth degree.
We played together a half-dozen times on rinks in
different parts of Moscow and beyond, and even
though I could never understand his banter between
teammates, I always knew that he was vouching for me
whenever I walked, unannounced, through the players'
close-knit hockey world. Yuri and his wife lived with
their adopted grandson — a series of shocking deaths
had affected their immediate family — in a small
apartment that they hoped to trade in for a larger

space, courtesy of the Russian Sporting Federation. But because Yuri was never a star of Yakushev's rank, he was low on the totem pole when it came to state support of retired athletes, and despite being the most active rec hockey–playing old-timer of his generation, and an ambassador of sorts, there was a good chance he might never move buildings. Still, Yuri had a good attitude. When I asked him if he was bitter about modern athletes making millions in the new Russia, he said, "I have a good wife, a good family and a good life. Besides, only a fool counts other people's money."

I hadn't remembered Blinov from '72 — certainly not as well as other players I met while visiting Russia: Maltsev, Gusev, Yakushev, Ragulin, Lutchenko and Anisin, with whom I spoke Italian (he'd been allowed to play there as a perk for years of service to the Russian game). If my memories of Blinov were inexact, his impressions of the series were like a sequence of ever-shuffling Polaroids. He remembered going down Yonge Street to buy albums as a reward for winning in Montreal in Game One ("I bought an album by Tom Jones," he told me), but had a hard time recalling other circumstances surrounding the event. Even though he was in excellent shape, something about the passing of time had weathered the old forward, and, after hearing him tell long stories that made little historical sense, I started to wonder about the effects of post-concussion syndrome and his ability to carry on living a normal life in spite of these injuries. Still, his seasoned face and slow way gave him a muted charm, and neither he nor any of his teammates ever looked at me sideways. I owe a lot to the Bleener for making our time among the Russian players seem easy. I knew what they were thinking whenever I showed up at the rink: "If he's good with Yuri, he's good with us."

By the time the Bleener — wearing number 9 and playing right wing with the crafty Maltsev at centre — jumped on the puck to Dryden's left with about five minutes left in the second period, the score stood at 4–3 for Russia. Knowing what we know now, another Russian goal — on top of the one they would end up scoring near the end of the period — might have been enough to maintain their lead through the game, giving the home side the series win. Then again, what happened next proved that, no matter how big of a lead the Russians might have carried into the final twenty minutes, it wouldn't have been enough to stop Team Canada from coming back and winning the series, a fate that is revealed in the game's details.

If Blinov was destined to fail on an opportunity that he'd magically created out of nothing, then Phil Esposito would become the single greatest force in denying one of the best teams ever — after playing one of their greatest periods ever — the ability to close out their opponent. The shift was Blinov's finest of the series. At one point, he twirled near the side of the net to get a clear shot on Dryden, flummoxing the Canadian defence. Moments later came a second shot, which he buried into the goaltender's stomach. Then, after a face-off, and a turnover at the blue line, the puck was swept back in the Canadians' zone, only to find Blinov's left winger, Vladimir Petrov, standing along the opposite boards. As the Canadian team skated towards him, Petrov passed the puck through a thicket of bodies, hitting Blinov just a few feet in front of Dryden. Watching the video now, the tall goalie's notion about goats and heroes resonates, more so considering that, as Blinov moved towards the goal, Dryden jumped to meet him, only to be juked out of position. Blinov curled the puck around his pad towards the net, which waved as empty as a wind socket.

After sliding the puck in, the Bleener swerved behind the goal and shot his arms into the air. Thousands of Russian fans in the arena did the same; untold millions followed suit. But something happened in that filament between ecstasy and despair: Esposito reached in, his arms fully extended, and bladed the puck away just as it was crossing the line. The certainty of the goal had been taken away, forcing Blinov into a crushing pose: back bent and stick resting on his knees, shaking his head in disbelief. I've watched the tape countless times to see if the puck crossed the line, but the evidence is conclusive in spite of the blurry old video stock: Espo kept the puck out. In the end, maybe the Bleener grew his hair long not only because his wife found it alluring, but because he thought it possessed special powers. After all, Espo's play seemed to carry the properties of luck and magic, although it was probably as much the result of energy and hard work. The Big Wop had that going for him, too.

By the time the period ended, Russia scored again

to make it 5–3. They'd seized control of the play and had shot in front on the scoreboard, adding to the immense pressure on Team Canada. Canadian TV showed us Pat Marsden interviewing Leafs legend Syl Apps ("After this, our hockey will never be the same"), then Bill Good and Howie Meeker sounding concerned as they talked about what they'd seen. In Russia, the broadcast fell to black with somnambulant classical music playing quietly in the background. This was common for Soviet hockey broadcasts, even games of this magnitude. "The Russians didn't do intermissions," said Ralph Mellanby. "They never did a pre- or post-game, either. Sometimes they did news between periods, and sometimes they did opera, but they never did interviews or analysis. Personalities were never ascribed to the players; you never heard their voice, never heard them talk about the game. It was quite the opposite from what went on at home, when anyone could talk about how horseshit the team was playing. After Game Eight — the greatest game ever in the history of Soviet sport — their broadcast simply ended. They returned to their regular programming."

We Are More Interested in Gags

As a child, legendary *Montreal Gazette* cartoonist
Aislin (a.k.a. Terry Mosher) had Alan Eagleson —
the series' architect, Bay Street lawyer and former
NHLPA felon — as his babysitter. Around the same
time, Mosher's dad took him by streetcar to where
the Richard Riots were happening outside the Forum,
giving him an eyewitness view of the rise of Quebec
nationalism as it played out on the ravaged streets of
his city.

Before the '72 series, Mosher was contacted by
publisher Jack McClelland to work on a book about
the event. "Jack asked me to come to Toronto," he
remembered, "to talk about it. I was thirty years old
and had been drawing for a while for the *Gazette*.
We met at the Park Plaza rooftop bar — Margaret

Atwood was there, and some other writers — and he got me a ticket to Russia as part of a tourist package that included Rocket Richard. I was credited as a photographer because there's no way the Russians would have let a political cartoonist into their country. That said, I wouldn't have known an f-stop from a bag of weed. Instead, I just drew. At one point during my trip, I managed to meet with the editor of *Krokodil*, the humour magazine that was part of *Pravda*, the state newspaper. After looking over my portfolio, he asked me, 'So, the papers in Canada actually print this?' He was amazed what could be allowed in the press, and when I asked him if he'd let me work for them, he pushed the drawings back across the table, and said, 'Well, here we are more interested in gags.'"

Mosher said that the Rocket was "mostly a shy, quiet man and he relied on me a little because I was one of the few people around him who could speak French. But at the airport, neither of us said anything because we couldn't believe what we were seeing: old women in kerchiefs cleaning with sticks and brooms. Coming towards us was a whole phalanx of Chinese men dressed in Mao drab. We shook our heads at the sight of them, and they did the same. There

were about 3,000 Canadians at the airport that day; everyone in hockey jackets and silly hats. I think the Russians expected us to be mild and docile, which is why our behaviour at the rink was such a shock. I later found out that the reason they'd let us behind the Iron Curtain was because it was supposed to be a trial run for a visit by Italian soccer fans a year later. We ended up being more than they'd bargained for."

Terry remembered sneaking out at night from his hotel, "basically trying to get arrested," he said, in search of a story beyond just the games. "I smoked pot and drank a lot back then and had long hair, and I was kind of fearless when it came to exploring the city. Before one game, I went out to the stadium and climbed to the top of the rafters. I watched the KGB and the police scour the arena, checking everything. It was menacing seeing them down there, all of these officials, not soldiers, straight from the offices of the Kremlin."

Another time, Terry and a few photographers met a quartet of Russian women on a city bus. "They found us amusing and so we hooked up with them," he said. "Then, as we were walking down the street, these guys shot out of nowhere and took the women away. We followed them to a special security room in the hotel and waited outside for awhile. A few days later, I saw one of them in Red Square. I talked to her and she told me to just go away. We got the message. We didn't want to ruin anybody's life.

"The funniest thing that happened to me at the rink was when Phil Esposito wanted to beat me up," he said. "After Vancouver, I'd done a cartoon with Espo as Gulliver tied down by the other players with the line, 'How's that for teamwork, Phil?' written on it. Jack McClelland pulled out the cartoon and showed Phil during practice, and, having not read Jonathan Swift, he didn't see it as being either very funny or pro-Espo. Jack gestured at me and said that I was the artist, at which point Phil called me over. He said, 'I don't want that fucking cartoon printed.' I told him that it was too late because it had already run a few days ago in the *Gazette*. He was livid. He told me, 'I'm gonna wipe the floor with you, you long-haired son of a bitch faggot!' I flashed him the peace sign — which is something he'd done from the penalty box a few games earlier — and the rest of the team cracked up. Later, I went to a hat shop near Red Square, and the woman asked me what I thought of Russian players. I told her that I thought they were very good, and then I asked her what she thought of the Canadians. She pressed her hands together like she was dreaming and she swooned, 'I love Phil Esposito!' I gave her an autograph of his that I'd collected before. She was so thrilled that she gave me the hat."

The Internet

With a handful of minutes left to go in the second period, announcer Brian Conacher invented social media in Canada. He told viewers, "Just a reminder to hockey fans at home who are watching these games: you can participate in voting for the most valuable player on Team Canada by sending the name of your choice to Box 5050 in Toronto, Montreal or Vancouver. The winner as selected by the fans will receive the Labatts Best-on-Ice award. Ballots are available from any Labatts representative."

Nobody Had to Die

As the clock fell and the period ended, 14 million Canadians — three-quarters of the entire population — did whatever they were supposed to do after finding themselves staring from a crumbling precipice into the brooding crevice of fate. Maybe some people scribbled the name of their MVP on a beer mat before sending it to their Labatts representative, but I doubt it. Instead, a collective emotional atrophy seized the country: hearts and minds and bodies sore and exhausted while pressed to couches and bar stools and upholstered car benches. In our small Etobicoke gym, my friends and I were too spent to play war. Instead, we collapsed to the floor, stoop-shouldered and cross-legged, as aware of the unknown as any other time in our young lives. André Brin of Hockey

Canada noted that one of the most unsettling, and impactful, things about Game Eight was the fact that it was the first time kids of our generation had ever seen adults behave so emotionally in public and at school. Teachers were freaking out, as groundless as any of their charges. Musician Stephen Stanley said, "A few years after '72, my teacher admitted to me that he was, more or less, hammered during Game Eight." Some people have compared the events of September 28, 1972 — and its effect on Canadians — to the JFK shooting in Dallas. But, as Gord Downie once told a Boston radio announcer, "Only in our case, nobody had to die."

Writers are challenged on where to start when it comes to describing the stunning events of the third period of Game Eight because, in Canada, there was no reference point — no template — to the relentless drama and surging gusts of passion that were played out in full view. In the USA, the confrontational and emotionally fraught birth of their country — to say nothing of VE Day, the moon landing, "Who Shot J.R.?" and 9/11 — affords citizens a scale by which historic events can be measured. It's even truer in the case of sport, which, to many Americans, is about a battle of will and superstars whose achievements are expressions of pure individualism. But when Canadians talk about someone like Bobby Orr — who practised with the reserve players on the day of Game Eight, hoping against hope to get into the final match — rarely is he identified as a symbol of our national character. Instead, we see Bobby as a shy kid from

Parry Sound, Ontario, who was just really good. It wasn't until '72 that people started talking about the game in terms of what it said about who we were and where we were going. And even then, it was as much a celebration of character as a study of how the team's lawless behaviour had let our society down.

Before 1972, Canada had never been centre stage in any international event of any significance — less so when it came to sport. If the Soviets had dominated the Olympic Games, and the USA and Britain — our cultural, social and political cousins — produced star athletes from Jesse Owens to Roger Bannister to Wilma Rudolph to Muhammad Ali, in Canada it was Ethel Catherwood this, Bruce Kidd that. These athletes inspired us, but they were unknown outside of the country. The only Canadian athletes recognized abroad were hockey players — in some cases, they were the only *thing*; Lightfoot and Medicare and the Robertson screwdriver and the toboggan be damned — and, going into the third period of Game Eight, it looked as if they were about to be defeated by a country of dark shadows with 131 million people to Canada's to 21 million. You'd have excused us for feeling like all was about to be lost. Without hockey to define us, we would have nothing. We would cease to exist.

But just as he'd done in every other crucial moment of the series, Phil Esposito met these concerns head-on. Striking quickly and authoritatively, he slapped the puck past Tretiak after taking a pass from Peter Mahovlich, who'd fallen into the end boards like a man over a barrel before slinging the puck to the front of the net. Canada pushed out a great gust of breath. Jack Ludwig, writing in *Hockey Night in Moscow*, reported that if there had been a certain amount of playful and good-natured ribbing among Canadian and Russian fans over the previous games, all of that changed once the fourth goal was scored. Ralph Mellanby said, "I'd never seen a press corps so united over a single event." The face-painted fans roared at their opposites, waving fists and shaking flags and screaming epithets about beer and snow and freedom and Canadian Tire and

Stanfield underwear and the Reversing Falls and the Guess Who. Ludwig wrote that along the perimeter of the rink, "Walkie talkies sent out the call, and, in half a minute, a huge detachment of police came trotting in." Ralph Mellanby added, "As the game went on, there were more and more soldiers, their numbers multiplying with each period. You could see it. You could feel it. Things got a lot more intense."

Volga Lightning

For Trent ("Bill") Frayne, the esteemed sports writer, the pressure of covering the event proved to be too much. During Game Eight, Frayne decided that he needed a drink. It was partly the working conditions that brought this about: prehistoric teletypes with Cyrillic letters, old clunking typewriters and curious sets of eyes on curious faces watching him as he wrote from a dry-heated room in the bowels of Luzhniki Arena, trying to meet his transcontinental deadlines. Frayne had been sober for a few years, having watched his friends and peers sink a little too deeply into the sportswriters' distress of long nights and endless bars that were the homes away from home to toy department scribes. But considering where he was and what he was doing and the fact that everyone else had found comfort in black market Armenian brandy and red pepper vodka, he stuffed his hat on his head, left the press box and headed for the stand-up bar at the end of the runway.

Around the beginning of the third period, Frayne soundlessly asked the grave-looking attendant for a drink — pantomiming a tip of the wrist — and was poured a plastic cup of Volga Lightning. Staring into the clear spirits, he might have paused for a moment to ask the Gods of Temptation for forgiveness when, out of the stumbling blue, fellow scribe Jim Coleman grabbed him by the nape of the neck and shouted, "You won't believe it, Bill! Broadway Rod Gilbert's getting into a fight!" The drink rippled in its cup as the two sportswriters ran back to the press box.

They Spun Like Maple Keys

Gilbert Rod and Yevgeni Mishakov slugged wildly at each other, spinning like maple keys to the ice. Hewitt shouted, as if suddenly electrified, "You can feel the tension almost everywhere!" After climbing to his feet, the Russian player — twice as wide as Gilbert and with a face like a shovel — discovered that his nose had been bloodied, while the Canadian — soft-featured and dashing to the point that he'd been the subject of an Andy Warhol litho — rose unscathed, if more muss-haired than anyone had ever seen. Mishakov gestured at Gilbert to come at him again, but the Canadian turned away. It was the right thing for the usually uncombative player to do, having gone to a dark, new place in an effort to motivate his teammates, a gesture that meant more to Team Canada than the Russians.

It's often the effect of the fight that matters more than the fight itself, and, in this case, it helped trigger two of most epochal moments in Canadian sports history. Broadway Rod had forced a crack in the levee. After this, anything was possible.

A New, Terrifying Presence

Such was the epic and complicated nature of the 1972
series that almost every player on both teams will
be remembered beyond a single defining moment.
Because each game was informed with the intense
focus of two nations, every shift mattered and every
mistake counted, to say nothing of important goals
that have since become sewn into the fabric of history.
One of these was the short-handed goal scored by the
tall, gangly forward Peter Mahovlich in Game Two
in Toronto, as important a match for Canada as the
last three of the series. The Little M — as effective a
player as his older brother, Frank, but never as prolific
a scorer — had high cheekbones and a Fred Gwynne
forehead. His eyes were like two great plums set into
the gaunt landscape of his face, and during play, they

widened to full capacity. With Canada killing a penalty while leading 2–0 in Game Two, he grabbed the puck on the good side of the blue line after a bank pass from Esposito. Stickhandling irreverently towards a lone Russian defender with great sweeps of the blade, he freestyled while moving down the ice. Approaching the player, he raised his stick for a slapshot, and then, in a perceptible moment of intelligence and cunning, froze it as it came down. The defenceman, who'd stilled himself to block the shot, was left flailing as the Little M wound past him towards the goal, where Tretiak slunk in the cold of the tall forward's shadow like an animal sensing a new, terrifying presence. Mahovlich held the puck out, then drew it in, then moved it to his left, then to his right as Tretiak's eyes trained on the hypnotic biscuit as if he were a child at a carnival shell game. But because the goalie had been busy concentrating on the darting puck, he'd failed to move far enough out of his crease, and soon, Mahovlich was on top of him, his wingspan extended, knees hiked in stride. The Little M pushed the puck past Tretiak, who'd dropped to cover the lower half of the goal. Skate-stepping out of the crease in joy, he was engulfed in a press of his teammates' sweaters.

Some people have called it the greatest short-handed goal ever scored. Considering when it happened, how, and for whom, they wouldn't be wrong.

Peter Mahovlich's next great moment of the series came six games later, with the score tied 5–5 and seven minutes left to play in Game Eight. This time, what he did had nothing to do with scoring, but everything to do with victory. Yvan Cournoyer had pulled Canada into a tie after a screaming, tape-perfect pass from Brad Park to Phil Esposito, who'd controlled play in the Russian zone before the Hab forward backhanded the puck over Tretiak, having fallen, once again. Despite the puck tickling the loose webbing that hung at the back of the Russian net, the goal judge sat unmoving, refusing to turn on the bulbous, red onion-shaped light in recognition of what was an obvious score. The referees huddled to discuss what to do, but that there was any discussion at all ignited something in series organizer Alan Eagleson, who bounced out of his seat. At the time, people assumed that the Russians would refute the goal as a way of fixing the result — after all, the on-ice official had made his decision — but Brian Williams saw it another way. "I thought what

Eagleson did was wrong," he said. "He reacted out of suspicion of the Russians, rather than what they were."

Scuttling down the wooden steps to confront the goal judge at ice level, he was grabbed by one soldier and then another until black-coated KGB agents appeared out of the shadows, sensing an opportunity, perhaps, to punish one of the boorish visitors, which they'd been keyed to do ever since Team Canada arrived in Russia. Eagleson tried to wrest himself free, his elbows snapping the air, but the soldiers pinned one hand behind his back, then reached for the other while marching him towards an exit at the end of the rink. All of this was happening. All of this was real.

As his team celebrated their goal, Peter Mahovlich looked to the other side of the ice. Maybe he saw something with those great, plum-shaped eyes, or maybe he heard something. After the television replay showed the goal once, then a second time, they came back live to a shot of about a half-dozen Canadian players stooped over the boards, and a single figure on the other side of those boards: Peter Mahovlich. From film stock shot by a roving camera crew for the purposes of a documentary, Eagleson can be seen being dragged away just as the enormous forward comes into view, his stick thrust at the soldiers like a joust. At first, Mahovlich confronts them from his knees, having tripped over the boards, but then, as he stands, Brobdingnagian on his skates, the soldiers release Eagleson. "They had guns, but we had hockey sticks," said Espo, years later, shaking his head at the memory. Whatever the nature of the weaponry, something terrible was poised to happen under the low arena lights, but, then, something didn't. Peter Mahovlich had diffused an incident that could have tarred the entire event, and if Bobby Clarke had acted shamefully in breaking Valeri Kharlamov's ankle or J.P. Parise had nearly killed a referee or the Canadians' immature behaviour reflected poorly on the country whose colours they were wearing, let it be stated that what Mahovlich did defined his team, too: an act of courage and loyalty, one friend coming to another friend's rescue. After releasing Alan Eagleson, the young Russian soldiers — if not the Red Guards — also looked relieved that Mahovlich had stepped in. The poor bastards just wanted to cheer on their team like everyone else.

Eventually, Eagleson — along with translator

Aggie Kukulowicz — jumped the boards in their Dack's and blue Team Canada blazers and were shepherded across the ice to the bench by the rest of the team, who'd rushed to the scene along with Sinden and Ferguson. While crossing the rink, the series' organizer pistoned a middle finger at Kremlin officials, including Brezhnev, who sat on high from the far end of the arena, and whom it was forbidden to film. Trainer "Frosty" Forristall walked beside Eagleson at the front of the procession. In some respects, the corpulent Bruins trainer was the occasion's perfect hood ornament, despite being of American descent. For the average Canadian, it was in Frosty — big-assed, beer-bellied and long-haired — that they saw themselves, and were they in his shoes, they probably would have done as he did: one finger on each hand raised in the face of every dirty Commie watching in the rink and at home. He returned to the bench with the rest of the team, the heat of their gaze melting the white ice. Sure, Henderson scored, and sure, it would become the most famous moment in Canadian history. But regardless of how the game was won, after Mahovlich's fearless leap, the Soviets were done.

The Insubordinate

Arthur Chidlovski had watched the incident on
Russian TV. He later remembered an interview with
Eagleson where he was asked what his gesture —
the one-finger salute — meant. Arthur said, "There
was no reference for this in Russia. Giving someone
the finger meant nothing to us." Eagleson told his
interviewer that it meant number one, as in "Team
Canada is number one!"

So, when Arthur got to visit the USA after
perestroika, he found himself at the customs desk
at LAX. "They asked me how many bags I had," he
said. "And so I held up the number one, the way
Eagleson had. You can imagine what happened next.
They saw me as an insubordinate and took me away
into this room, where they drilled me with questions.

I explained the whole story of Eagleson to the customs official, but he was Mexican-American. He wasn't much of a hockey fan and, of course, he had no idea who Alan Eagleson was."

A Wild Stab for It

We all know what happened after Cournoyer's tying goal and Mahovlich's rescue. But there were other moments that came before Henderson's 34-second beauty that informed the game's remarkable conclusion. For instance, on the shift after the tying goal, Phil Esposito — whose series performance quoted equal parts Louis Prima, Pagliacci, a Mafia don, your Uncle Umberto, Primo Carnera and Enrico Caruso — drove his stick into the side of Vladimir Petrov as they collided in the Russian zone. The play was blown dead, and after Brian Conacher told the whole of Canada, "I have to believe that, right now, Phil Esposito is playing the greatest hockey of his life," the Big Wop skated towards the heckling crowd, smiled his best fuck-you smile and raised his arms in the parody of a goal celebration. Then he kicked his skates together and gave the Russian fans a mock salute. The referee called for him to return to the face-off circle and he did, but not before waving his hands at the crowd in disgust. Studying the anatomy of all of the plays in reverse of Henderson's series-winning goal, one thing is clear about Team Canada and their spiritual — and, it would turn out, points — leader. They were loose — very loose. Show me someone who can joke around and pantomime and be a total goof while their nation's moral, spiritual and cultural destiny is on the line and I will show you but one man.

Espo.

Before the winning goal, both teams were forced, for a moment, to play four on four hockey: Dennis Hull and Petrov sent to the box with coincidental minors. If Team Canada had been gaining strength with time, the extra skating over open ice seemed to drain the energy of every Russian player except the indefatigable Yakushev, who was Espo's equal save for the yucks. Russia's lack of zip was a stunning reversal from the series' early days. In one sequence, Boris Mikhailov, the team's gritty and determined centreman, skated at Pat Stapleton on the blue line

only to curve away from him like a slow-moving shopping cart — a mere suggestion of effort. Near the end of the game, it was as if some players had simply granted Team Canada possession of the puck after sensing that, in the end, winning would mean more to Sinden's charges. For the Soviets, performing as well as they had against the best of the NHL meant

that they'd already won the battle, even if they'd end up losing the war. They'd made a historic statement, showing the world the great beauty and power of their game, and, to this day, when the Russians talk about what happened in Montreal, their memories are sugared with the surprise of their remarkable triumph in Game One. But in the late stages of Game Eight, if the Canadians were skating for their junior coach, their immigrant grandparents and the boys back home in their favourite wood-panelled bar, the Russians — who had grandparents and coaches and hometown bars, too — drew from a lesser emotional store, their hearts and minds burdened with the dead weight of playing in the name of political ideology. They may have proven that puck possession, an emphasis on skill and pure speed made for a more aesthetically pleasing and dynamic game, but they also proved that feeding the engine of the soul with dogma can only make you skate so hard. Ideology may have brought their team together, but it couldn't lift them. In the end, the Canadians came back to win the series not necessarily because they were better, but because they were freer. At least that's how it seemed.

At 1:48 of the final period, there was a face-off in Canada's end to the left of Ken Dryden. Esposito won the draw, then got the puck to Peter Mahovlich, who spotted Cournoyer racing up the ice. The Little M lifted the puck into the Russian zone, but the Roadrunner narrowly missed it: offside Canada. Josef Kompalla pedalled the puck back to where the face-off had been before, and while the Russians lined up, the Canadians waited a moment. Esposito called together the other five players on the ice — all of them Montreal Canadiens — and organized them into a small huddle, something that had never been done in NHL hockey. The puck dropped. Espo won the draw again.

Guy Lapointe flipped the puck into the Russian end, and the Russians dished it out. Peter Mahovlich found it at centre ice and threw it back into the zone. Cournoyer chased, but came up empty, and the Russians dished again. The puck kicked around in the neutral zone, only to be scooped up by Yakushev who, as he had all series, rushed into the Canadian zone, protecting himself by throwing out his shoulder. But Serge Savard, as if he'd been waiting for the opportunity all series, drilled the square-shouldered winger into the corner. The puck popped loose. Esposito, back-checking in the depths of his zone, headed behind his net, whacked the puck over to Cournoyer, and the Roadrunner sliced it out. Lapointe changed for Pat Stapleton as Vasiliev retreated, racing to get to the quick black dot.

He threw the puck to Liapkin, who lost it along the boards. For a moment — maybe two moments — the screen went black. When the image returned, it was to find Cournoyer at centre ice along the far boards. The Roadrunner chipped the puck into the Russians' zone. A Soviet defenceman cleared it up the wing, only to have Cournoyer, who'd followed the flight of the puck, intercept it along the boards inside the Soviet blue line. Peter Mahovlich came off — or was called off by Henderson, according to the other players — and was replaced by the eventual goal scorer, who stood directly opposite from Cournoyer.

The puck slid on a diagonal to the streaking

Henderson. He made a wild stab for it. And fell. Esposito, coming out of nowhere, took a shot at the net while turning away from the goalie. Tretiak saved, but on the rebound, taken by Henderson, he failed to tamp the puck. Just as the disc was spinning under him, Espo was turning, too. Out of his single revolution: an explosion of pure joy and happiness. One man leapt into another man's arms who leapt into another man's arms. Then, they were all doing this. And that was Game Eight, live from Russia.

Notes on the Photos

Endpapers: Fans await the return of Team Canada.

Page 6: A Team Canada supporter in Moscow.

Page 9: Harry Sinden.

Page 18: Phil Esposito in Moscow.

Pages 22-23: Ken Dryden covers a Valeri Kharlamov rebound.

Page 33: Esposito addresses the media and a nation.

Page 39: Bobby Clarke.

Page 44: Alexander Ragulin.

Page 50: The Soviets in Toronto.

Page 57: Alexander Yakushev.

Page 79: Viktor Kuzkin wearing a Canadian welcome gift.

Page 91: Fans at the Luzhniki Ice Palace in Moscow watch from behind the iron fence.

Pages 104-105: Espo "salutes" the Soviets.

Brian Pickell is a musician and photographer with several books to his credit, including the official Hockey Canada history of the legendary 1972 Canada-Russia series. He lives in Paris, Ontario.

At ECW Press, we want you to enjoy this book in whatever format you like, whenever you like. Leave your print book at home and take the eBook to go! Purchase the print edition and receive the eBook free. Just send an email to ebook@ecwpress.com and include:

- the book title
- the name of the store where you purchased it
- your receipt number
- your preference of file type: PDF or ePub?

A real person will respond to your email with your eBook attached. And thanks for supporting an independently owned Canadian publisher with your purchase!

Get the eBook free!*
*proof of purchase required